Leading Your
Sports Team

John C. Maxwell
Leadership Books for Students

(Based on *Developing the Leader Within You*)

Leading from the Lockers:
Student Edition
ISBN 0-8499-7722-3

Leading from the Lockers:
Guided Journal
ISBN 0-8499-7723-1

The PowerPak Series

Leading Your Sports Team
ISBN 0-8499-7725-8

Leading in Your Youth Group
ISBN 0-8499-7726-6

Leading at School
ISBN 0-8499-7724-X

Leading As a Friend
ISBN 0-8499-7727-4

"These books are outstanding. John Maxwell's leadership principles have been communicated in a way that any student can understand and practice. Take them and go make a difference in your world."

—DR. TIM ELMORE,
Vice President of Leadership Development, EQUIP;
Author of *Nurturing the Leader in Your Child*

Leading Your Sports Team

by

John C. Maxwell

with

Mark Littleton

Tommy nelson
Thomas Nelson, Inc. • Nashville

POWERPAK SERIES: LEADING YOUR SPORTS TEAM

Based on John C. Maxwell's *Developing the Leader Within You.*

Published in Nashville, Tennessee, by Tommy Nelson®, a division of Thomas Nelson, Inc.

Special thanks to Ron Luce and Teen Mania for providing research materials for this book.

Unless otherwise indicated, Scripture quotations are from the *International Children's Bible, New Century Version,* copyright © 1983, 1986, 1988.

Scripture quotations marked (NKJV) are from THE NEW KING JAMES VERSION of the Bible, copyright © 1979, 1980, 1982, Thomas Nelson, Inc., Publishers.

Library of Congress Cataloging-in-Publication Data

Maxwell, John C., 1947–
    Leading your sports team / originated by John C. Maxwell; adapted by Mark Littleton.
        p. cm. — (PowerPak collection)
    ISBN 0-8499-7725-8
    1. Leadership—Religious aspects—Christianity—Juvenile literature.
[1. Leadership—Religious aspects—Christianity. 2. Sports—Religious aspects—Christianity.] I. Littleton, Mark R., 1950- II. Title. III. Series.

BV4597.53.L43 M39 2001
248.8'3—dc21

                                                              2001030743

Printed in the United States of America

01 02 03 04 05 PHX 5 4 3 2 1

Contents

1

Lead Your Team to Victory! (Yes, You!)

God may be calling you to lead right now! Yes, you! He may have plans for you to someday lead your church, your community, your country. *What are you going to do when He calls? Panic?* See if He'll ask someone else? But God won't accept no for an answer. He'll expect *you* to lead.

How will you know what to do? By learning to lead *now*—in every part of your life. The great thing is that you don't have to be born a great leader, you can *learn* to lead. That's right, leading is a skill. God doesn't always choose great leaders. He chooses good people whom He makes into great leaders.

You may think, *I'm just a kid. Who'll follow me?*

With God's help, you may be surprised who'll follow you. There have always been young leaders. Look around.

Maybe you think, *But why should I want to lead? All it will give me is a headache!*

You're right! There are headaches that come with being a leader. Solving problems can be hard. You're dealing with arguments, keeping temperamental teammates in line. But there are also high payoffs for those who lead. Among them:

- ☐ Respect from friends and fellow team members
- ☐ The satisfaction of a job well done
- ☐ Possibly being the leader behind a winning team
- ☐ Academic and sports awards
- ☐ The preparedness and possibility of leading others later as an adult

Ultimately, the most respected, most remembered, and most revered people are our leaders. People like Michael Jordan, Kurt

Warner, and Sammy Sosa are not only players and play makers, but also leaders in their communities. Michael Jordan supports charities and is well known as a community-minded leader. Kurt Warner has helped fellow players on the Rams find Christ and demonstrates his Christian lifestyle in his community by speaking out against drugs and illicit sex. Sammy Sosa, slugger for the Cubs, often speaks in his Hispanic community of his commitment to helping young people excel, both in and out of sports.

So, whom do you look up to most? Whom would you most like to be like? I'd guess it's the leaders in your sports teams and in the pros.

Choosing to Be a Leader

I remember the first time I ever thought about being a leader. I was in the second grade, and a bunch of us decided to play baseball at recess. Two guys announced they would be captain and began choosing sides. I got picked—but for the wrong team. We began to lose badly and play carelessly. I was disgusted they didn't care. I decided something then, at eight years old. I determined I was going to make choices on what I was going to do, where I was going to go, and who I was going to team up with. I am sure this came from a very competitive spirit. Sometimes I am too driven. At the same time, that experience was good for me. That was how and when I decided I was going to be a leader.

Get Me a Leader! Quick!

Situation 1: You're standing in a locker room. Two guys on the football team have been ragging on each other all day. Suddenly, a fight breaks out between the two. Several guys try to stop it. They pull the two fighters apart. But they're both making threats, and everyone believes this will happen again.

Question: Would you like to be the kind of person who can step in and solve this problem before the fight? Would you like to be the one to help your team move on and beat other teams instead of beating up on each other?

Situation 2: You're ready to bat for your softball team. The other team is winning. It's a tight game. But no one has any ideas except to hit away and score. As everyone talks and listens to the coach, an idea pops into your head. You noticed the center fielder had trouble with flies to her left side and liners up the middle. No one else has noticed this.

Question: What would you do? Speak up and possibly be wrong? Or stuff it, try to hit to that spot, and see what happens?

Both of these situations call for leadership. Someone to **STEP IN, SPEAK THE RIGHT WORDS,** and influence others to take a new path—one that will take them to success.

Who wouldn't like to be captain of the team? Or the basketball point guard who calls the plays? Or the girl the coach points to and says, "Do it like her"?

Leaders are the most essential element of any sports team.

○ Without leaders, the team gives up.

○ Without effective leaders, the team disbands.

○ Without enthusiastic, committed leaders, the team never gets into the game.

But with good leaders—Wow!—anything is possible!

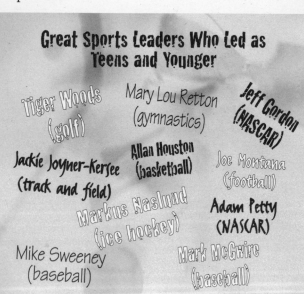

Great Sports Leaders Who Led as Teens and Younger

Tiger Woods (golf)

Mary Lou Retton (gymnastics)

Jeff Gordon (NASCAR)

Jackie Joyner-Kersee (track and field)

Allan Houston (basketball)

Joe Montana (football)

Markus Naslund (ice hockey)

Adam Petty (NASCAR)

Mike Sweeney (baseball)

Mark McGwire (baseball)

Christian Walk or Balk?

Consider, too, your Christian walk with Jesus. His first priority is making you like Him. What then does He want you to become? A fisher of men (and women). A bearer of the fruit of the Spirit. A leader who plays well and tells the truth. A man or woman of God after God's own heart.

You could be known for all those qualities.

What Will Being a Leader Do for Your Christian Walk?

☐ Help you become more like Jesus (Romans 8:29)

☐ Make those you lead want to hear your Christian testimony (2 Timothy 4:2–5)

☐ Give you opportunity to grow spiritually as you learn to help others (1 Timothy 4:16)

☐ Make you bold for the kingdom of God (Colossians 4:2–6)

☐ Open doors that might otherwise be closed (Revelation 3:8)

And if you are a leader on the ball field, court, or track, your friends are more likely to listen to you as a Christian.

"Please, Lord, send someone else!" —Moses to God (Exodus 4:13)

Great. We need leaders. But who? The truth is that nearly anyone has the potential to be a leader in a sport in which he has a strong interest. It could be you. God may not call you to be president of the United States, or commissioner of baseball, but He might nab you for a stint as a genuine leader your friends follow on your soccer, field hockey, volleyball, golf, football, or baseball team.

MARK 1:17: JESUS SAID TO HIS DISCIPLES AND ULTIMATELY TO EVERYONE WHO WILL EVER FOLLOW HIM: "COME AND FOLLOW ME. I WILL MAKE YOU FISHERMEN FOR MEN."

You never know. God has a way of picking people who don't look real fantastic at the time, but as He develops them, they—like Jesus' disciples—Peter, James, John, and

Andrew—become excellent leaders because of God's presence and influence in their lives.

Leaders Who Are Made Don't Fade

You might think, **But I'm not a born leader!** *It's really hard to step up to the front of the group.*

I'll tell you a secret: We all think that about ourselves.

Consider Josh. Not a natural leader, certainly not born into it. His swim team was failing. His team members were ready to give up before they'd even gotten wet. They were smaller, shorter, and less mature than their opponents.

> "LIFE IS LIKE A TEN-SPEED BIKE. MOST OF US HAVE GEARS WE NEVER USE."
>
> **—CHARLES SCHULTZ,**
> **CREATOR OF PEANUTS**

Everyone said it couldn't be done. Then Josh stood up in the locker room, feeling a little tug in his heart from God. "My brother always beat me at everything," he said. "He was a natural athlete. But one day we were in the pool, and he wanted to race. I don't know what happened. I had a motor on or something.

But I beat him. He couldn't believe it. He went on to beat me the next time and the next. But that one time—I won. I'll never forget it. That's what we can do here. We just need to go for it like it's the only one that counts."

That galvanized Josh's team. Everyone went out of that locker room ready for combat. After that, Josh was a natural. But he didn't start out that way.

Josh wasn't a born leader. But God put him in that locker room that day with that idea, and it turned things around. If God wants you to be a leader, He'll give you the equipment to pull it off.

Be the King of "One Thing"

You don't have to be great at everything, just one thing. To become a leader you need to discover that one thing and work on it. Perfect it and use it for your team's glory, and your teammates will applaud you.

As you develop yourself, people will notice. And sooner or later, if you're faithful, God will give you an opportunity to lead.

Be watching. Because He's watching you.

2
Leadership Is Influence

Okay, you'd like to be a leader. But where do you start? Perhaps with a definition. What is leadership? Ask ten people and you'll get ten definitions. Here's one I like: **Leadership is influence.**

If you can influence people to change, to support a plan of action, or to hunker down to go for a goal, you're a leader. If people are following you, you're a leader. It's the guys who think they're leaders when no one is following who are mistaken. My favorite saying about such people is, "He who thinketh he leadeth and hath no one following him is only taking a walk."

"Hey, Someone's Following me!"

If you want to lead, you need followers. Without followers, leading is meaningless. Leading means you must have someone who says, "Let's go for it. I'm on your team!"

But how do you get followers? In a word: *influence.* As you talk about your plan, as you outline the plays, as you spur your teammates on toward a victory, you're influencing them. And as I said: Leadership is influence.

Did you know we all influence someone? Even you. Which baseball player hasn't rallied a

How to Influence Others

- ☐ By a compliment or a word of encouragement
- ☐ By a special sign of support—a touch, a note
- ☐ By applause and cheering
- ☐ By presenting a solid plan of action
- ☐ By rallying when people are down
- ☐ By coming up with a new idea that works
- ☐ By citing the truth

slumping batter with a shout from the dugout: "Just connect, man. That's all we need!" What soccer player hasn't spurred her team on after giving up a goal when she cries, "Shake it off! The next one is ours!"

Influence Isn't Influenza

Everyone's life is filled with moments when he has been influenced by another person—for better or worse.

You Never Know Who's Going to Jump on Your Wagon, So Be Prepared to Pull

What kind of influence you have will depend on what kind of relationship you have with God. David Robinson, who plays basketball for the San Antonio Spurs, has made millions as a star in Texas. For many years, he believed he was a Christian. He attended church as a kid, but his commitment to Christ was rather detached.

One day, a friend, evangelist Greg Ball, visited in David's home. He sat down with David and asked some pointed questions. Then HE TOLD DAVID HE NEEDED A HEART FOR GOD. David was stunned, and pinned to the wall spiritually. He now says of that moment, "Greg really convicted me that day, and that day I made a commitment to the Lord."

Since then, David Robinson has been influential not only in the game of basketball but also in the kingdom of God. He has changed the face of the world more through his Christian witness than anything he could ever do as an NBA star.

For instance, several years ago, David and other NBA Christians organized and spoke at a huge rally in San Antonio, called "Jammin' Against the Darkness." More than eleven thousand men and kids showed up at San Antonio's HemisFair Arena. Many received Christ as they listened to the inspired speaking of the NBA stars and others. It became the biggest crusade ever offered in San Antonio.

When You Invest in the Future, You Get Lots of Presents

The question before any person seeking to lead is not *whether* you will influence others. You will. For good or bad. What you need to settle is *what kind* of influence you will be.

For instance, below is a joke about a basketball player and a football player that shows the dark side of influence:

The basketball player ran down the middle of the interstate against traffic, yelling, "Eighty-eight! Eighty-eight! Eighty-eight!"

A football player, stopped on the side of the road with a flat, called to him, "Hey, what's going on?"

"Come on, it's fun," the basketball player cried. "Try it."

The football player joined him. Soon they were both running down the interstate yelling, "Eighty-eight! Eighty-eight! Eighty-eight!"

Soon, a Mack truck barreled toward them. The basketball dude shouted, "Don't stop."

The football guy didn't, but when the truck was almost upon them, the basketball player jumped out of the way. Meanwhile, the football player was flattened.

The basketball player looked at his "friend" sadly, then continued on down the highway, shouting, "Eighty-nine! Eighty-nine! Eighty-nine!"

The sad thing is how many people act just like those two. Some regard certain sports as only for dummies (football, wrestling) while other sports can be played only by intelligent people (basketball, gymnastics). Such attitudes can destroy teams and the fun of a sport. You can influence people best by caring about them, helping them, and being their staunchest supporter—even when everyone else is shouting for their heads.

A high school baseball player named Tom took the plate in a championship game with two outs, two men on, and down by one. A solid hit would score a run and tie the game so they could continue to fight, or score two runs and win.

As Tom readied himself for the pitch, suddenly

the sun hit his eyes. He swung poorly, chipped the ball into a pop-up and an out.

Game over.

Tom felt like a jerk.

Another guy on that team named Joe cared about Tom and stopped by his locker after the game. "SUN GOT YA, huh?" Joe said as Tom banged around in his locker.

"How did you know?"

"Same thing happened to me last year. It's a killer."

"What did you do about it?" Tom asked.

"I went home, knelt by my bed, and said, 'Thanks, Lord. Next time I'll do better. But I know You're in charge, so I'm not going to worry about it.'"

"Really?"

"Yeah, it helped a lot."

Joe just went about his business after that, but his words stuck with Tom. Later that night, Tom also hit his knees by his bed and thanked God for teaching him something new that day.

YOU CAN'T ALWAYS WIN. You can't always be number one. BUT YOU CAN TRUST GOD for everything. Joe exercised influence on Tom at that moment, and I don't think anyone would disagree that it was a very good influence.

Got a Fish? Don't Let It off the Hook

If you're like me, you probably want to influence your friends and team members for good, for God, for building God's kingdom. That's the first and best step to becoming a leader. God will use you on your team and in your sport.

You might think, *Hey, I'm no David Robinson or Jeff Gordon.* Or maybe, *Jackie Joyner-Kersee was great. But who am I?*

You are a child of God, and one whom God will use—if you let Him. **YOU CAN BECOME A SOLID, GOD-GLORIFYING LEADER ON YOUR TEAM,** if you simply apply several skills and make them part of your life.

The Three Levels of Leadership

☐ Position—the coach says, "Follow him because I say so. And if you don't, I'll bop you one."

☐ Permission—the team says, "We will follow him because we respect him. Plus, he has a very good bop."

☐ Production—everyone says, "This guy knows how to get us there. Let's go. Or I'll bop you one."

In Monopoly, You Start at Go! In Leadership, You Start at Low!

Over the years, I have seen three distinct levels of leadership. The lowest is what I call POSITION. You are the leader because of your appointed position. Maybe the coach made you captain and told everyone you're the man. Maybe the team elected you before they really knew you personally. Maybe you're the oldest girl on the team so you get the spot.

2 TIMOTHY 1:7: GOD DID NOT GIVE US A SPIRIT THAT MAKES US AFRAID. HE GAVE US A SPIRIT OF POWER AND LOVE AND SELF-CONTROL.

Regardless of the reason you got the position, that's all it is: a position. You're the leader not because of talent, but because of a title. The primary hazard of this situation is that people follow you because of your position, nothing else. They will never do more than they're required to do because they may not even respect you. POSITIONAL LEADERS HAVE TROUBLE MOTIVATING OTHERS when they're not being paid to play or work. Many times, if you're not very good, they'll just quit.

Coach Barbara always appointed a player to be captain of the girls' soccer team. One year, she selected Lisa, largely because Lisa was Barbara's niece. Lisa found it tough going. The team members would listen to her only because she was the appointed captain, but they talked behind her back and didn't respect her. The coach had made a big mistake with that appointment. And Lisa also made a mistake in accepting the position.

However, LISA COULD HAVE MOVED TO THE NEXT TWO LEVELS by showing her leadership skills to her teammates. Starting out as a leader under these conditions is often the way it happens, and there's certainly nothing wrong with it. Just make sure you move on to the next two levels.

Positional Leadership in the Bible: King Saul

The children of Israel cried out that they wanted a king. God sent Samuel the prophet to anoint Saul. He was a handsome man: tall, strong, and determined. King Saul became king by God's decree. He was appointed king, the perfect example of leadership because of position.

But King Saul was not faithful to God and ultimately committed suicide. Why? Because he never really rose above position. People followed him more out of fear than love. And in the end, he not only lost all his material possessions, he lost his soul.

You're the Man!

The second level of leadership is **permission**. In this situation, members of the team follow you because they know you care, they know you know your stuff, and they know you're good at what you do. They "permit" you to be leader by gladly following.

Leadership by Permission in the Bible: David

Like King Saul, David was appointed king. He was the youngest of many brothers and not considered king material even by Samuel the prophet. But it was Samuel who, under God's direction, anointed David to be king. But David soon proved himself, first by defeating Goliath the giant and second by leading the armies of Israel to many great victories. Men followed David because they loved him and would die for him. Why? Because they knew he loved them and would not lead them into ruin.

David also failed, though, when he committed adultery and then murder. His position was king, and most still followed him. But he was a crippled leader because of his sin. And that is a serious matter in the eyes of God.

An old saying is that people don't care how much you know until they know how much you care. The leader in this situation cares, and so people follow. He or she leads by relating to the members, getting to know them, hearing their concerns, and trying to put the good ideas into practice. The followers know they have a voice, because the leader listens to each one of them as an individual and as a team.

Give the Girl a Chance!

Jenny was elected the captain of the girls' basketball team because she was a good player and knew how to score points. **THERE WERE SOME GRUMBLERS** who felt Jenny should not be captain, but they decided to give her a chance.

After the election, she made an effort to talk to every team member. She found out what they needed, what ideas they had, what strategies they would use to win. **ON THE COURT, JENNY DIDN'T HOG THE BALL.** She passed to those who were open and called plays that gave everyone an opportunity to score. In time, there were no grumblers on that team. Jenny was leading because she had permission, not just because she had a position.

Shooting through the Hoops

The level to strive for in leadership is the third one. I call it **production**. At this level, the leader, now being followed by permission, can start to make things happen—good things. Morale goes through the roof. The team chugs along making a real mark. Being on the team is no longer a grind, but fun.

This should be the goal of every leader, to get into the position, win the permission of his teammates, and then begin producing. There's a joke about a rooster who happens upon a goose egg. It's huge compared to the chicken eggs he's used to seeing, so he pushes it back to the coop. There he gathers all the hens and says, "I'm not complaining. I'm not comparing. I just want to show you what is being done in other places."

Just as that rooster wanted to motivate his

> 1 TIMOTHY 4:12: YOU ARE YOUNG, BUT DO NOT LET ANYONE TREAT YOU AS IF YOU WERE NOT IMPORTANT. BE AN EXAMPLE TO SHOW THE BELIEVERS HOW THEY SHOULD LIVE.

Leadership by Production in the Bible: Jesus

Jesus gained His initial position of leadership the same way King Saul and King David did: God the Father appointed Him. After Jesus was baptized, God spoke from heaven and said, "This is my Son and I love him. I am very pleased with him" (Matthew 3:17). He just couldn't contain Himself.

Jesus began building relationships and soon had many disciples of which twelve became the core. He told these men if they followed Him, He would make them "fishermen of men." These men left everything to be with Jesus. They "permitted" Jesus to be their leader and were utterly loyal to Him.

As Jesus performed miracles, spoke words of life, and carried out many deeds of love, He became the classic "productive" leader, the One people followed because they believed He was the Son of God and would take them places they could never go by themselves. In this respect, Jesus is the classic leader who went through all three levels and excelled in each. Today, people all over the world follow Him.

hens, so the leader at the production level motivates, encourages, builds confidence, and guides. He leads the team to new heights of accomplishment simply by being a producer.

JEREMIAH 29:11: "I SAY THIS BECAUSE I KNOW WHAT I HAVE PLANNED FOR YOU. . . . I HAVE GOOD PLANS FOR YOU. I DON'T PLAN TO HURT YOU. I PLAN TO GIVE YOU HOPE AND A GOOD FUTURE."

What level are you at? Maybe you're not even at level one. And that's okay. WE ALL START SOMEWHERE. As you climb the leadership ladder, remember the principles.

So **HOW DO YOU GET TO LEVEL THREE** with your teammates? Read on! You'll soon know the secrets of getting to level three . . . and how to stay there.

3
Priorities:
Setting Your Sights on the Right Goals

Goals Make it Fun

Goals are powerful motivators. When we have them, we are more focused and we have more energy. When we don't, we get easily distracted and fail to accomplish much of anything. I remember the first basketball goal my father got me, as a kid. He brought it home and began to put it up in our driveway. I could hardly wait to play.

It grew dark, and my father wasn't able to

finish putting the rim up on the backboard. He told me he would finish it later in the week, and went inside. I was so excited, I couldn't wait to play. So, I picked up my basketball and began shooting it up at the backboard, trying to imagine whether it would have gone in. It was difficult. I needed the rim. Within three minutes, I set the ball down and didn't pick it up until the goal was up. Goals are what make sports fun. The same is true in life and leadership.

If you aim at nothing, you will always hit it. In football, that's so true. They call it "intentional grounding." In baseball, it's also true. They call it a "walk." In hockey, it's definitely true. They call it a "free-for-all."

Everyone knows that any sports contest has a specific goal. Cross the goal line for a touchdown in football. Score tens in the compulsories in gymnastics. Reach the end of the pool with the fastest time in swimming. To play effectively, you must try to reach your goal and score the points to win. You can strategize. You can sacrifice smaller goals to reach larger ones (as in a sacrifice fly in baseball). You can work down by down to get to the goal line, and you can take a long time doing it if you want, or accomplish it all in one incredible pass.

The goal is the measure of what you want to achieve. If you reach the goal, you've achieved it. If you haven't, you've failed.

But what happens when you have no goals?

Have you ever played tennis without a net? Have you ever played baseball where people just practice hitting or catching, but there's no score?

It's frustrating, isn't it?

Why? Because **we want to reach for something.** We want to achieve something.

A primary function of a leader is to set goals and then think up ways to reach them. It's really as simple as that. If you learn to set goals and set out to accomplish them, you will be far ahead of most leaders.

Don't Throw Air Balls

The way to set attainable goals is simply to prioritize your day, your month, your year, even your life.

If you can prioritize, putting the most

important items on your "Top Ten" list of things to do today or this week, you'll make some major strides as a leader. It's when you let a lot of little, unimportant things bog you down that you lose the battle.

Biblical Goals God Has for You

God has some goals He wants to accomplish in your life. What are they?

- [ ] Bring you to faith in Christ (John 1:11–12)
- [ ] Make you into a true disciple who tells others about Christ (Matthew 28:18–20)
- [ ] Develop you into a disciple (2 Timothy 2:2)
- [ ] Make you like Jesus (Romans 8:29)
- [ ] Take you to heaven and have you reign with Jesus forever (John 14:1–3; Revelation 3:21)

Organize or Agonize

When you begin goal-setting, remember that you need to organize yourself. Don't be like the man who had written on his tombstone: "Organized at last." You don't want to have to wait that long!

No, organizing is rather simple. Just take out a piece of paper that you can keep in your pocket. First, brainstorm and then list everything you need to do that day. Don't prioritize yet; just list everything you can think of to do.

Once you've done that, **SELECT THE FIVE TO TEN MOST IMPORTANT ONES** and number them in order of importance. For example, your initial list might look like:

☐ Practice swinging bat a hundred times

☐ Work on line drives

☐ Clean locker

☐ Talk to coach about ideas

☐ Work with Bill on his curve ball

☐ Take out the dog

☐ Finish chores at home

☐ Have quiet time with God

Looking at the list, which ones would you say are most important?

I'd select items like this:

7. Practice swinging bat a hundred times

6. Work on line drives

5. Clean locker

8. Talk to coach about ideas

3. Work with Bill on his curve ball

2. Take out the dog (because the dog needs it!)

4. Finish chores at home

1. Have quiet time with God

Look at that list. Maybe you've got it on notebook paper, a sticky note, or toilet paper, but the important thing is that suddenly you are ORGANIZED! You have some goals to strive for. You have something that makes your day worth living through. You're actually going to DO SOMETHING today!

Now all you need to do is figure out how to do what you need to do, and you're almost there.

Choose or Lose

Ultimately, what this comes down to is making choices. You must choose between what is

Sports Legend: A Little Choice

Bo Jackson played defensive end in high school. His team didn't excel, though, and his senior year the team went 3–7. When Bo went to Auburn University, he continued in that position but was a backup for the running backs. When all three running backs had health problems, the coach asked Bo to "fill in." He made the choice to do his best. He went on to become one of the best running backs in football history.

good and what is better, between what is better and what is best. Good things are always good, but are they the best things for you at this time and in this place? You should pray about this and seek God, but you also must use your mind and heart to determine what is best for you at any given moment.

PSALM 90:12: TEACH US HOW SHORT OUR LIVES REALLY ARE SO THAT WE MAY BE WISE.

If you don't choose your own priorities, someone else will. Remember the adage "Idle hands are the devil's playground." That's true. When you have nothing to do, you can be sure the enemy will sneak in and show you some trouble to get into. But when you make wise, godly choices, God is honored and you will be praised, loved, and honored.

What Does God Want from Me?

Of course, the ultimate question for any Christian is, "What does God really want me to do?"

Principles for Knowing God's Will

☐ Does the Bible give me any specific guidance? Do I know a verse or a story or something else that can help me in this decision?

☐ Have I prayed about it and asked God to give me wisdom? He promises that He always will (see James 1:5–6).

☐ Have I consulted with others and gotten their wisdom on the subject?

☐ Has anything happened or is anything now happening to indicate what God might want?

The problem of knowing God's will is an old one and not easily answered. But to make a determination, you can follow a few simple principles.

Lyin' Around with Lions

Have you ever seen a lion tamer at work? What are the things he takes with him into a cage? Usually a gun and a whip, but anything else? Yes, you've got it, a little chair with four legs. Did you know this is the most important thing he takes into that cage? Why? Because to "tame" those lions, he will stick the stool in their faces with the four legs sticking out toward them. The lions in turn will try to focus on all four legs, but they can't, and a kind of **paralysis strikes** in which they are overwhelmed and back down.

People use this tactic in sports all the time. A blitz in football is meant not only to down the quarterback, but also to throw utter confusion into the offense. A "full-court press" in basketball does the same thing—the other team is trying to make the defenders lose focus.

That can happen with your goals, too. If you lose focus, if you feel overwhelmed, if you don't prioritize, you will become paralyzed and unable to achieve anything. But if you focus on what's important and what's urgent, if you set out to deal with those problems first, undoubtedly you will achieve great things.

JOSHUA 1:8: ALWAYS REMEMBER WHAT IS WRITTEN IN THE BOOK OF THE TEACHINGS. STUDY IT DAY AND NIGHT. THEN YOU WILL BE SURE TO OBEY EVERYTHING THAT IS WRITTEN THERE. IF YOU DO THIS, YOU WILL BE WISE AND SUCCESSFUL IN EVERYTHING.

4
Integrity:
You Are What You Do

Elaine and Steffi were talking about the captain of their soccer team, Niki. They liked her, but Elaine said, "I just never know whether she's telling the truth."

"Why?" Steffi asked.

"I caught her in a lie once. In a way, it's ruined everything."

It happens. When we do wrong—sin—we make it more difficult for our team members to follow us. Why? Because they don't trust us. Trust is the result of integrity. Without integrity there is no trust.

Have you ever heard the expression "What you are shouts so loud I can't hear what you say"?

It's true. You can shout all you want, but if you lie, cheat, steal, backstab, gossip, or do any number of other wrongs, you will never lead. People do not follow someone they can't believe in and trust.

How do you build trust? Through integrity. By always doing what is right. And when you do make a mistake, by admitting it and asking for forgiveness.

It's really that simple. HONESTY IS NOT A TRICK OR A STRATEGY; IT'S A LIFESTYLE.

1 THESSALONIANS 4:11-12: DO ALL YOU CAN TO LIVE A PEACEFUL LIFE. TAKE CARE OF YOUR OWN BUSINESS. DO YOUR OWN WORK … IF YOU DO, THEN PEOPLE WHO ARE NOT BELIEVERS WILL RESPECT YOU. AND YOU WILL NOT HAVE TO DEPEND ON OTHERS FOR WHAT YOU NEED.

Integrity is not so much what we do as who we are, for who we are determines what we do.

High Standards or a Low Life?

How do you build integrity into your life? By maintaining high standards. When the team works out, do you pretend to perform, or do you give it your all? When the coach calls for attention, do you laugh and keep on talking, or do you look him in the eye? When you're called upon to do a job on the team, do you do it with gusto, or just passably?

Integrity calls for high standards. If you lower them, everyone else will, too. When you lead by example, you must maintain a high example, or everyone else will follow your poor example—and ultimately you will all fail.

Well-Rounded Players Needed

One year out of high school, I came home and visited with my high school basketball coach. In our conversation, he said something I never forgot. He said, "John, you were a great player—but you could have been so much better, if you were well-rounded." When I got a puzzled look on my face, he continued. "John, you were a great offensive player, you made the all-conference team. If you would have learned to play defense, you could have been all-state."

The same is true in life and leadership. When my life is incomplete and part of it is underdeveloped, I lose some integrity with others. Furthermore, I don't have the respect I could have from others, either. In our leadership and our lives—we must become well-rounded. We must learn to play both offense and defense.

People Who Led by Example in the Bible

☐ As David was mighty before the Lord, so he raised up men who were mighty (see list in 2 Samuel 23:8–39). Like leader, like follower.

☐ Paul told his readers to imitate him as he imitated Christ (1 Corinthians 11:1). People did what he did because he did what Christ did.

☐ Jesus washed the disciples' feet and told them to do the same to their disciples (see John 13). Hey, it may be a stinky job, but you can put a clothespin on your nose, if necessary.

How to Break a Camera

Today, people talk in "sound bites," and they work to project a certain "image." That image is what the press says so-and-so is like. But God sees the truth about who you are. And so will your followers. Jesus' disciples followed Him to the point of death because He obeyed His Father to the point of death. Like leader, like follower.

> PROVERBS 10:9: THE HONEST PERSON WILL LIVE SAFELY. BUT THE ONE WHO IS DISHONEST WILL BE CAUGHT.

Don't Play Politics

Have you ever heard of people who are good politicians on sports teams? They're the ones who get elected, make big promises, and then don't deliver. They're often braggarts who think making themselves look big and important is the way to make it as a leader.

But such people rarely have integrity.

Image without Integrity
Destroys Followers

A Jewish boy loved his father and went to synagogue each Saturday with his family. But when they were forced to move to a new town, there was no synagogue there, so the father announced they were leaving their Jewish roots and attending a Lutheran church because it would be good for business. This confused and angered the boy. He began to see capitalism as the real ruler in people's lives and religion as a mere "drug." He grew up to become the father of Communism. His name: Karl Marx.

They're the ones who will run down other team members when the coach isn't within earshot. **THEY'RE THE ONES WHO** will **COMPLAIN** about a losing streak **BUT DO NOTHING** about it. They're the ones who try to get loyal team members cut from the team just because they may not have as much talent.

But it's the person who shows real integrity who wins rightly and righteously. That person will emerge as a true leader others want to follow.

Live and Speak the Truth

Make this resolution right now—if you want to be any kind of leader: "I will live the truth, not just talk about it." Say it out loud. Say it proudly.

If you will do that, you will please your followers, your coach, and God. You will become on the outside who you are on the inside.

" I BELIEVE THAT FOOTBALL, PERHAPS MORE THAN ANY OTHER SPORT, TENDS TO INSTILL IN MEN THE FEELING THAT VICTORY COMES THROUGH HARD, SLAVISH TEAM PLAY, SELF-CONFIDENCE, AND ENTHUSIASM THAT AMOUNTS TO DEDICATION."

—DWIGHT D. EISENHOWER, THIRTY-FOURTH PRESIDENT OF TH UNITED STATES.

5
Changing without Losing Your Jersey

It has been said, "There are three kinds of people: those who let it happen, those who make it happen, and those who wonder what happened."

Put yourself in this situation:

Your parents announce to you they're moving the family to another state. Your dad has received a big promotion. For you, it means another soccer team and a whole new set of problems and people.

How do you deal with it?

Change Is a Penny from Heaven

Change is a constant in life. Most Americans move once every five years. Teachers come, teachers go. Young people advance from elementary school to junior high and then high school and college. All of it means THINGS WILL CHANGE IN YOUR LIFE.

How do you handle change? How do you help others to change in the midst of difficult circumstances and situations?

A leader is a change agent. A leader helps himself or herself change and also helps others to make changes in their lives.

Check Your Motives

When I joined our varsity basketball team, I felt I had something to prove. I wanted to score as many points as I could. It made sense at the time. After all, isn't scoring points going to help the team?

The answer is both yes and no. In my case, I

was scoring points for myself more than doing it for the team. My motives were wrong. My senior year, I decided that winning was more important than individual statistics. I made a big change. It worked.

My junior year, I scored more points. But my senior year, we won more games. We went all the way to the championship, and I won the "Sportsmanship Award" for the school. I guess both coaches and players noticed the change and how it helped the team.

Change: Resist or Insist?

Most people resist change to some degree. They don't like moving from their comfortable, known situation to a possibly uncomfortable, unknown one. As a result, people resist change. In the situation on page 47, if your family is moving, chances are that you will be moving, too.

Change will happen whether you like it or not. Resisting it brings its own set of problems. Why not be a leader and get involved in making the change happen?

Peter

Peter wanted to be like Jesus, but he had to go through some tough times to learn how much he really needed to change. When Jesus was about to die on the cross, Peter told the Lord that he would fight to the death anyone who tried to hurt Jesus. Jesus in turn told Peter that three times that very night he would deny he even knew Jesus. Peter fought the idea of his own cowardice, but Jesus was right. Peter made the denials. Afterward, when he realized what he'd done, he went out and "wept bitterly." But Peter changed. He repented. He knew he couldn't do it on his own. The next time we see Peter before a crowd he is preaching the gospel, and three thousand people are converted!

Change Is Attitude

How, then, do you bring about positive change in your life and the lives of others?

First, you have to want to change! If you don't want it, it will never happen.

For instance, **David Robinson,** star center for the San Antonio Spurs, attended the Naval Academy on a basketball scholarship. He was content to warm the bench his freshman year, not really exhibiting much commitment to his sport. When he played, though, he excelled. Some people around him saw greatness in the making, but it was being wasted by a who-cares attitude.

One day, David's coach, Paul Evans, spoke with him about what he saw in the young man. Evans said, "You could become one of the game's best players. But you have to want it. And you'll have to work."

That little "pep talk" changed David Robinson's life. Today, he is considered one of the greatest centers of all time.

But he had to "want" it.

Are You Happy?

Sooner or later you have to ask yourself: **Am I happy with things as they are?** Do I want to do better? Do I want to excel? Do I want to go all the way?

If so, then change is the means.

Warming Up to Change When Everyone's in the Arctic

Do you trust people? Do people trust you? Is there someone who has betrayed your trust? Trust is important in leadership. **Trust doesn't happen overnight.** It is built by the small and large things you do and say every day. Eventually, someone will trust you. Will you be worthy of that trust? And, someday, you will trust someone else. Without trust, you will go bust.

But what if you trust someone who isn't trustworthy? It happens. Some people are not trustworthy. Some have good intentions, but still break your trust. In both cases, that person will have to rebuild his trust with you. He'll have to start small, and it will be a long time before you will trust him with something else. The same goes for you, if you break a trust.

GALATIANS 5:16: LIVE BY FOLLOWING THE SPIRIT. THEN YOU WILL NOT DO WHAT YOUR SINFUL SELVES WANT.

A second thing you can do is to change yourself before asking others to change. Are you the

The Right Response

A young man had made it to a championship game, but the umpire was messing it up. The ump seemed to be making all the wrong calls. In previous games, the boy had argued with other umps and in one case had been thrown out of a game. He'd been advised to "cool down" and "give a respectful answer." In this final game, the boy stood up to the plate, and on the fourth pitch he struck out without swinging. The boy began to argue with the ump, and the ump said, "I know I'm right because I have my rule book right here!" The boy remembered his coach's words to "cool down." He decided to nod and walk away. At the dugout, his coach said, "Good move! We need you in this game."

classic pot calling the kettle black? As Jesus said, do you have a stick in your eye, and you're telling your friend about a speck of dust in his? Do you have a problem with gossip? Don't go screaming at others about it (or gossiping about them!).

No, control your tongue first. Then maybe you can cool the gossipmongers with a word from the Scriptures.

From Nobody to Somebody: Moses

When God called Moses to go back to Egypt and help free Israel from slavery (see Exodus 3–4), Moses tried every excuse in the book: "I am not a great man! Why should I be the one?" "What if the people say, 'What is his name?' What should I tell them?" And, "Please, Lord, send someone else."

1 CORINTHIANS 15:58: STAND STRONG. DO NOT LET ANYTHING CHANGE YOU. ALWAYS GIVE YOUR-SELVES FULLY TO THE WORK OF THE LORD. YOU KNOW THAT YOUR WORK IN THE LORD IS NEVER WASTED.

GOD finally ORDERED HIM TO "CHANGE," and he did— quite unwillingly. Over the next few months, Moses watched as God unleashed His power on Egypt, sending ten plagues that had frogs leaping out of cooking pots and flies biting them. Moses came to truly trust God and believe He knew what He was doing. In the end, Moses became

Shortstop Didn't Stop Short

In the 1990s, Cal Ripken, star shortstop for the Baltimore Orioles, was having problems hitting. His old stance and swing were no longer working. His batting coach stepped in and helped him find a new stance that looked awkward and difficult to Cal. But he tried it, and his hitting improved, so much that on the night he broke Lou Gehrig's long-standing record of most consecutive games played, Ripken hit a home run. There, he revealed two important leadership qualities: being consistent by showing up every day to play, and hanging in there, even when things aren't going well.

one of the greatest leaders in human history, enabling more than three million Jews to escape Egypt and go to a new land. He was the classic ordinary-guy-makes-good.

6
Problem Solving:
Fixing What's Broken, Healing What Hurts

Everyone faces problems—big ones, little ones, medium-size ones. Some anger us. Some slay us. Some we just tromp over like a tank going over a barbed-wire fence.

The thing you should always remember is that as a Christian, you have the greatest problem solver of all time already on your side. Jesus solved the problems of death, sin, eternity, heaven, hell, and everything else by doing what He did on the cross and rising three days later. THAT SAME JESUS LIVES IN YOU.

You should expect that His creative and imaginative power will be available to you as you try to solve problems like the ones above. He may not fix the precise problem you have, but He will give you the attitude and commitment to stay strong despite the problem.

As a leader, what would you do in these situations?

1. Katie comes to you and complains about Betsy, who has been hogging the ball on the basketball court. Katie's a good player and shooter. She says, *"BETSY IS JUST A GUNNER."* But the coach says nothing because Betsy does score points. What would you recommend Katie do?

2. Brad is in a batting slump. He's talked to just about everyone and it looks as though he will be **CUT FROM THE TEAM.** Brad finally comes to you and tells you being cut will be the worst thing that has ever happened to him. What do you tell Brad?

As a leader, you might advise Katie to hang in there while you talk to the ball-hogger. With Brad, you might want to remind him that there are many worse things than being cut. Besides,

Solving Human Fickleness

Elijah had a problem in 1 Kings 18. The people of Israel followed false gods. How could he prove to the people of Israel that there was only one God, and He was far more powerful than any man-made idol? He challenged the prophets of Baal (the idol) to a duel. Each side prepared a sacrifice (a bull on an altar) and then called on their god to incinerate it without them providing the fire. The prophets of Baal danced, screeched, prayed, and even slashed themselves with knives. But Baal didn't answer.

Then Elijah quietly folded his hands and said, "Lord, answer my prayer. Show these people that you, Lord, are God." God answered with a lightning bolt that burned up the sacrifice and blew the people away. They immediately cried out, "The Lord is God! The Lord is God!" (see 1 Kings 18:37, 39). After all, what would you say?

Elijah creatively solved the problem.

being cut might help him. In junior varsity he'll have an opportunity to shine and to practice his skills. Then, next year, he'll be more likely to make the varsity team.

Beautiful Things in Ugly Disguises

You might think, *Oh, I have so many problems, I don't know what to do.* But problems can be actually good things in disguise. They give meaning to life. They also give us a chance to see God work in and through us. And they give us a chance to grow spiritually. What better combination of things can help anyone become a better Christian?

Winning Takes Confidence

When I played high school basketball, my coach decided to do something strange. He made the rims smaller, and made us shoot foul shots. He thought if we could make the free throws with a smaller rim in practice, we

Problem Solvers of the Bible

Noah—flood coming; built an ark

Jacob—wife unable to have children; prayed for God's mercy; wife got pregnant

Moses—people enslaved; freed them by sending plagues to captors

Joshua—land needed to be conquered; conquered it piece by piece until there was real peace

David—giant scaring the army; lopped off his head

Jesus—mankind lost; died for our sins; made it possible for anyone anywhere to become like Him

would surely be able to make them with a standard-size rim in the games. I talked to him after practice and told him it would hurt the team. After shooting just ten free throws, I became so discouraged that it had the opposite effect on me. I saw it happen to the rest of the team as well. After two weeks, I was proven right. The coach never reduced the size of the rim again. The smaller rim got, the smaller

our confidence got, and the more encouragement we needed. His plan looked good on
paper—but it forgot the power of confidence.

Got a Problem? Here's an Answer

I have found a five-step plan that works in
solving most problems.

It is:

1. Identify the problem.
2. Ask the right questions.
3. Talk to the right people.
4. Get the facts.
5. Get involved and help find a solution.

It works like this:

1. IDENTIFY THE PROBLEM. Figure out what
the problem really is.

Cal Ripken, who needed to change his batting
stance, and Brad, in the earlier story about the
danger of being cut, weren't hitting. For Cal, the
problem was defined as his not meeting the ball

straight on. That helped his coach lead him to the next step. For Brad, he might have had to endure being cut in order to learn some skills on a lower level. When you see the problem clearly, you can face it head-on.

> PSALM 27:13-14: I TRULY BELIEVE I WILL LIVE TO SEE THE LORD'S GOODNESS. WAIT FOR THE LORD'S HELP. BE STRONG AND BRAVE AND WAIT FOR THE LORD'S HELP.

2. ASK THE RIGHT QUESTIONS. If you don't ask the right questions, you might be trying to solve the wrong problem, or make the right problem worse.

What if Cal Ripken's coach had asked the question, "How's your marriage, Cal?" thinking Cal was worried about his marriage and that was why he wasn't hitting? There's nothing wrong with that. Maybe Cal's coach did ask it. But he had to ask other right questions: Why aren't you meeting the ball? Is it your swing? Is it your stance? Is it your attitude? Are you giving up?

3. TALK TO THE RIGHT PEOPLE. Scripture says there's wisdom in many counselors. It's true. Getting second and third opinions always helps.

Perhaps Ripken's coach talked to other

Pitcher Worth a Thousand Words

The pitcher wasn't doing well, literally getting shelled. The coach walked out to the mound, had a little talk with him, then walked back. The pitcher made it out of the inning, but the next time out, he gave up a home run. The coach walked out again, had another talk, and walked back to the dugout. Finally, the pitcher gave up another single and then a triple. The coach walked out to the mound, and the pitcher said, "But, Coach, I told you, I'm not tired." The coach replied, "Maybe you're not, but I am."

coaches and players and heard what they thought might be wrong. "Oh, I think Cal has problems at home." "I think Cal is washed up, past his prime." "I don't know; I noticed he's hitting a lot of pops, not meeting the ball properly."

4. GET THE FACTS. Study the situation and make sure you're sure what is wrong.

> "STATISTICALLY 100 PERCENT OF THE SHOTS YOU DON'T TAKE DON'T GO IN."
> —WAYNE GRETSKY, HOCKEY PLAYER

Cal's coach might have taped videos of Cal's hitting to see what was wrong, or studied him to get the facts.

5. GET INVOLVED AND HELP FIND A SOLUTION. Sometimes you have to try several things, but if you keep working at it, you will find the right answer. Remember: A failure is a person who doesn't get up after failing. A success is one who keeps getting up until he does succeed.

Using this five-step problem-solving process will undoubtedly help you in your team situation. I've seen it work many times in mine.

7

Attitude:
Got a Bad 'Tude?
Get the Right One!

When I speak at conferences, I often ask everyone to participate in this exercise:

Write the name of a teammate you greatly admire: _____

Write one thing you admire about him or her: _____

Strangely enough, the thing many people admire involves attitude. Is the person positive?

Forgiving? Patient? Gentle? Kind? Tough-minded? Strong-willed?

Is Your Attitude an Asset or an Upset?

Attitude determines how you will do in just about anything you try.

☐ If you have a give-up attitude, you will probably give up.

☐ If you have a never-say-die attitude, you will go on and probably perform well.

☐ If you have a we-can-do-it-together attitude, you will be the type to get all the team moving in the right direction.

☐ If you have a "we stink" attitude, you will probably be part of the stink.

You can't help but notice that Cal Ripken showed up to play more than two thousand two hundred times *in a row*. His attitude was well-known to his fans. He never boasted, never made a lot of noise about his accomplishments.

He just quietly went about doing his work with a positive attitude that said, "*I will never give up.*" And that attitude has won him high marks in baseball and in the community.

The truth is that it is highly improbable a person with a bad attitude will be successful most of the time, if at all. And make no mistake about it, we are responsible for our attitudes.

Give a 'Tude Its Due

During my junior year of high school, our basketball team was awesome. I played with some of the most talented players in the state. Many predicted we would go to the state finals that year. But we never did. Why? We never learned to play together. The seniors and the juniors on the team couldn't stand each other. So, the seniors would only pass the ball to other seniors. The juniors began to do the same thing. Our coach got so angry with us, he started platooning us. He would put the seniors out on the floor one quarter and the juniors the next. Unfortunately, when forced to play this way, we

Key Christian Attitudes

Faithfulness (Luke 16:10–12)

Hopefulness (Ephesians 4:4)

Forgiveness (Matthew 18:22)

Love (1 Corinthians 13:1–13)

Gentleness (Galatians 5:22–23)

Kindness (Galatians 5:22–23)

Peacefulness (Romans 12:18)

Happiness (Psalm 1:1–3)

Endurance (James 1:2–4)

never had our best team out on the floor. It was awful. We only won three games that year.

My senior year, we decided to put an end to the junior/senior feud. We played together. The sophomores even got some good playing time. Although it was a less talented team, we went on to win a championship. Never underestimate the power of attitude.

The Power of the Right Attitude

Many years ago, it was said that no one would ever run the mile in under four minutes. The ancient Greeks tried so hard to do this that they had lions chase runners to make them go faster. Unfortunately, this mostly kept the lions from going hungry.

Then in 1954 a man decided he would do it or die. Roger Bannister was his name. He defied everyone and ran the mile in under four minutes. Boy, was the lion that chased him tired! (Actually, it wasn't exactly a lion, it was his coach.)

You know what happened? A year after Bannister showed it could be done, thirty-seven other milers broke it!

How did Bannister do it? Bannister trained no differently. But his attitude and the attitudes of those thirty-seven others all changed from "It can't be done" to "I'm going to do it!" What is the altitude of your attitude? Are you shooting high enough? Or do we need to sic a lion on you?

Don't Let Feelings Manhandle You

Now, all of us will admit to having negative thoughts and feelings now and then. They seem to just come upon us. But we can't let them control us.

Change Your Attitude or Change Your Sport!

On one team, one member of the team was always naysaying everyone else. "It can't be done," he shouted at meets. "You'll never do it." Finally, one day the coach confronted him: "Change your attitude or change your sport."

It's true. The wrong attitude can catch fire and burn down everyone in sight.

How do you change your attitude? Here are six steps I've found that work:

1. **Identify problem feelings.** Be aware of any bad attitudes. Drop them like a rock.
2. **Identify problem behavior.** What are you

doing wrong? If you don't know, ask one of your parents. You can be sure your parents will tell you straight.

3. **Identify problem thinking.** What goes through your mind that you need to stop? *I'll never win. I'm a loser.* Refuse to think that way, or you will be that way forever.

PHILIPPIANS 2:5–8: IN YOUR LIVES YOU MUST THINK AND ACT LIKE CHRIST JESUS. CHRIST HIMSELF WAS LIKE GOD IN EVERYTHING. HE WAS EQUAL WITH GOD. BUT HE DID NOT THINK THAT BEING EQUAL WITH GOD WAS SOMETHING TO BE HELD ON TO. HE GAVE UP HIS PLACE WITH GOD AND MADE HIMSELF NOTHING. HE WAS BORN TO BE A MAN AND BECAME LIKE A SERVANT. AND WHEN HE WAS LIVING AS A MAN, HE HUMBLED HIMSELF AND WAS FULLY OBEDIENT TO GOD. HE OBEYED EVEN WHEN THAT CAUSED HIS DEATH—DEATH ON A CROSS.

4. **Identify right thinking.** When you do find some good, wholesome thoughts, work on strengthening them. Make those thoughts do push-ups and sit-ups till you're fit.

5. **Make a public commitment to right thinking.** Tell your teammates you're in a new frame of mind. It's win-or-die-trying for you from now on!

6. **Develop a plan for right thinking.** Put it on paper. Put the paper in your wallet and read it now and then.

Bad habits and bad attitudes are like weeds. If you

Keeping Your Attitudes Right

☐ Say the right words.

☐ Read the right books.

☐ Listen to the right CDs, radio stations, tapes.

☐ Be with the right people.

☐ Do the right things.

☐ Pray the right prayer.

And your heart and might will be right.

don't pull them while they're small, soon you have to have dandelion tea for dinner every night.

Work on your attitudes. Get them right— with yourself, with your team, with your Lord. And soon everything else will be right as well.

8
Relationships:
Are You a People-Eater or a People-Encourager?

Building relationships is key to building yourself as a leader. If you don't build relationships, and then keep building them, they will begin to break apart, distrust will mount, and the people you want to lead won't want to listen to you anymore—and that will destroy any possibility of being a true leader. Consider all the relationships that exist on the average football team in which you play halfback:

You and God
You and yourself

You and your family
You and the coaches
You and the team
You and the backfield
You and the quarterback
You and the offensive line
You and the defense

The average family of four **has twelve distinct relationships,** from you and your father, to you and all three other members. For instance, you have a relationship with your mom, your dad, and your brother or sister. That's three. Then there's your relationship with your mom and dad together, your mom and sibling together, and your dad and sibling. That's three more. Finally, there's your relationship with all three of them together. All of these are different and involve different dynamics. Then there are their relationships with you. It gets complicated, doesn't it?

The important thing is that **relationships make life worth living,** for it is through relationships that we learn, grow, love, give, serve, help, build up, encourage, and are encouraged.

God's Value of You

◻ He has your name written on His hands (Isaiah 49:16).

◻ He wants you to reign with Him (Revelation 3:21).

◻ He wants us to live in His house forever (John 14:1–3).

◻ He has stored our tears in a bottle (Psalm 56:8 NKJV).

◻ He has written our names in His book (Revelation 20:12).

◻ He forgets our sins (Isaiah 43:25).

◻ His Son died for us (1 Peter 2:24).

◻ He considers us His friends (John 15:14).

◻ He will give us an inheritance from His wealth (Ephesians 1:18–19).

◻ He has given us every spiritual blessing (Ephesians 1:3–4).

◻ He has given us His power (Ephesians 1:18–19).

◻ In Him we lack nothing (2 Peter 1:4).

◻ We are precious to Him (Psalm 116:15).

Wow! If God feels this way about you, how should you feel about your teammates?

A Worthwhile Relationship Is Worth Your While

One thing to ask at the start is, "How much do you value others?" Do you see not only how you can contribute to their lives, but also how they contribute to yours?

Read "God's Value of You" on page 77 for some insight into how God feels about you. Certainly it shows how much we should value each other.

Then think about how He values you and expects you to value others.

Live Life One "Yea" at a Time

Do you care about the people you lead? Are you an encourager? Do you step in when things look bad and say something positive like "Great job!"? Or DO YOU COMPLAIN and put down people with statements like "Get over it"? Do you care about the people you know? Pray for them? Show you love them by your actions?

Think about how you feel when people say to you:

☐ "Hey, you did a great job there today!"

☐ "That was a tremendous thing you did there."

☐ "I really appreciate your taking the time to tell me that."

Do you feel worthwhile? Good about yourself? Think about it. You, too, can impart that worth by a few simple words: the kinds of words that can make a person's day, week, or year! When you use encouraging words, you build people up, make them feel worthy, and strengthen their inner image of themselves.

Do you know one of the greatest ways to encourage someone? Just listen to him or her. Ask a question or two and let them take off! A good listener is always an encourager.

Make Them Feel Like a Million

Not everyone can be a champion. But anyone and everyone can feel valued when you let them know they play a part, they have an important role, they're making a contribution.

Have you heard the story of the gymnastics team made up of squirrels, rabbits, and ducks? The leaders trained everyone the same way. The squirrels were great on the balance beam, but not so good at tumbling, so they were forced to spend most of their time tumbling. The ducks were excellent on the long horse, taking great flights off it, but because they couldn't 'hand' well on the uneven bars, they were made to work on that all day. And the rabbits were excellent at tumbling, but they couldn't do the balance beam. So . . .

GALATIANS 6:1: BROTHERS, SOMEONE IN YOUR GROUP MIGHT DO SOMETHING WRONG. YOU WHO ARE SPIRITUAL SHOULD GO TO HIM AND HELP MAKE HIM RIGHT AGAIN. YOU SHOULD DO THIS IN A GENTLE WAY. BUT BE CAREFUL! YOU MIGHT BE TEMPTED TO SIN, TOO.

You get the idea. **THAT TEAM WAS MESSED UP.** What they needed was to accept their differences and work in the ways they were most suited. That's when things start to click for teams and individuals.

As a leader, you want to help people find their place. Then when they do, let them go for it for all they're worth.

In the Gym with Jim

Jim was a water boy for the soccer team. No one paid much attention to him, and many joked about him as being too fat to play. Jim just took it, being careful to put just enough ice in the water to make it last all afternoon and keep cold.

One very hot day, Jim didn't show up. Someone else took over as water boy, but he didn't put ice in the water. The water was warm. **Everyone complained**. Suddenly, the team saw Jim's value. The next week, Jim did show up. From that time on, no one talked about how fat Jim was, but rather about how cold and refreshing the water was and how much they liked it.

> "IF YOU DON'T KNOW WHERE YOU'RE GOING, YOU'LL END UP SOMEPLACE."
>
> —YOGI BERRA,
> BASEBALL PLAYER
> AND MANAGER

Do You Play or Do You Slay?

Of course, the main thing about most sports is that **whole teams have to work together** to make it work. Are you a team player? In basketball, do you let others shoot, or are you a gunner? In soccer, do you try to make *others* look good, not just yourself?

It's a matter of outlook and attitude. Are you going to build relationships to make a better team, or put down others when you don't get what you want? If you put down your team members, they're going to feel down in the real contest, and that won't benefit anyone.

One Bad Apple Is Rotten to the "Corps"

Of course, there will be times when you need to step in and deal with someone who is tearing down others or HURTING THE TEAM. In such cases, take the initiative. Be gentle. Be kind. Express yourself directly, but with a caring heart. Most people will listen under such conditions.

When you start to shout, put down, belittle, or manipulate, then you're in trouble.

You Need a Close Relationship with God

Luther Elliss is a star defensive tackle for the Detroit Lions. After suffering some serious injuries while body-surfing in California, he returned to the football field seeing double and triple, a problem from which he still suffers. It was at this time he kept returning to God for help. "I was surprised to be named to the Pro Bowl," he said. "I thought I played decently, but I didn't feel it was my best year. I was very honored and just praising God. He works in so many mysterious ways. Sometimes when we're not expecting it, He brings wonderful things into our lives." He added, "God's always been a very important part of my life. When I was in trouble, or struggling with something, or when I was afraid, I would call upon God."

Tempted and Tripped Up by Drugs

Elise was tempted one day and tried some illegal drugs. Soon, Elise was addicted. Her friend Sherry learned what had happened and went to Elise's house. There, she sat down with her friend and gently confronted her about the problem, saying **it would destroy her** if she didn't deal with it. Sherry suggested that Elise get into a drug program and that she would even go with Elise to the meetings.

Elise agreed. But notice several things about this confrontation.

☐ Sherry did it in private, not in public.

☐ She was gentle in her words, not accusing.

☐ And she offered to go through the process with her friend, the ultimate gesture of support.

Confrontations usually work when you're kind, gentle, and understanding, as well as willing to stick with the person. When you go in shouting, and showing anger and hatred, you've already lost.

Let God Be the Big Cheese

The most important relationship you have is with God. Without Him, you're done for. And so am I. He's the cornerstone, the linchpin that holds everything together. We ignore Him to our peril.

In this respect, there are several things you should do in this relationship. To start, share some quiet time with God.

1. Read God's Word. Daily, if just for a few verses.

2. Spend five minutes thinking about what you just read. Ask several questions. What is God saying to me in this passage? What things should I put into practice today as a result of what I've read? Is there a verse to memorize and store in my heart? Is dinner ready yet?

3. Spend some time in prayer. Keep a list. Pray specifically about needs, concerns. Pray for you, your team, your family, your church, your school. If you can, write down your prayers in a journal and look for God's answers. Expect God to answer, too. And when He does, thank Him. God appreciates a little gratitude now and then, too.

4. Get involved in Christian fellowship by joining a church, where love, friendship, and encouragement are practiced.

Do these things and God will be pleased.

9
Self-Discipline:
Sweating with the Best

Les was an all-state tackle on the high school football team. As a sophomore, people were saying he was NFL material.

But Les had a problem. Good as he was on the field, he also drank a lot of beer and partied into the late hours on school nights. His grades slipped. Because they admired him, other team members joined him in the party lifestyle. Eventually, their team finished the season with more losses than wins—all because one guy didn't have self-discipline.

Self-discipline is a key ingredient to success in a leader. If you're not disciplined, your team- mates won't be, either. If you party all night, so will they. If you drink, they'll think it's okay, too. So, besides disobeying your parents, the law, and God, you will lead your teammates to do the same dangerous thing.

Discipline That Builds Disciples

How do you build a disciplined lifestyle?

Start now. Don't wait till tomorrow or next week. Start this week, this morning, and stay with it. Get to practices on time. Obey the coach's rules. Be an encourager and motivator, all the time.

Start small. Don't try to do everything at once. Start with a few major disciplines and stay with them. Build on that foundation.

Follow these seven steps:

1. Get Organized or You'll Agonize

Start thinking about how to manage your day, your week. Make plans. If you fail to plan, you plan to fail. Get things in order. Figure out what to do and what time to do it. Organize your desk, your room, your locker. Refuse to let everything sink into a murky mess.

2. Set Your Priorities or They'll Be Setting You

Remember in chapter 3 you created a list and then numbered the items in order of importance? Start doing that daily. Brainstorm and list the top three things you have to do today and make them your priorities. You'll be amazed at how much it will make you feel that you've actually gotten something done!

3. Make the Dates before You Become Dated

Once you've gotten your daily priorities in order, start thinking longer term. Where do you want to be in a week, a month, a year, five years? Start putting those plans on a calendar.

"By senior year I want to be on the varsity."

"By the end of this year, I want to be first string."

4. Expect the Unexpected

Remember that you will be interrupted. Figure that as part of your schedule. Learn to deal with the guy who just wants to "talk" and the girl who wants to go out for a Coke after the game. Remember your priorities, but also remember people. There is no instance in the Bible where Jesus refused to help someone even though he or she interrupted His plans.

5. Take 'Em One at a Time

When you try to juggle many projects at once, inevitably the whole pile comes crashing down. You get discouraged. The pile lies unfixed.

But do one project at a time and you'll make progress. There's the little celebration after each thing is done. And

> "WHEN THE ONE GREAT SCORER COMES TO WRITE AGAINST YOUR NAME—HE MARKS—NOT THAT YOU WON OR LOST—BUT HOW YOU PLAYED THE GAME."
>
> —GRANTLAND RICE, SPORTS WRITER

there's the sense that you're going somewhere. Don't forfeit that sense of progress for some prideful belief that you can handle everything yourself. It will get you nowhere.

6. Develop Systems That Work for You

Some people like a notebook. Others, a calendar. Whatever you choose, develop ways of doing things that fit you. Is it best to have your quiet time in the morning? Then go with that. But if you're more of an evening person, there's nothing wrong with that style. If a to-do list is your preference, use it well. Remember: The best system for you may not work for your best friend.

> GALATIANS 5:22–23:
> BUT THE SPIRIT GIVES LOVE, JOY, PEACE, PATIENCE, KINDNESS, GOODNESS, FAITHFULNESS, GENTLENESS, SELF-CONTROL.

7. Be Character-Driven, Not Emotion-Driven

Are you the master of your feelings? When everyone's pigging out on pizza, can you say, "No, I have to stay in shape"? When other guys tempt you with beer or drugs, can you turn away or even run? When everyone complains that it's too hard, the coach is being too tough, do you suck up your gut and hang in there? If not, you're letting your feelings control you. Instead, let character be your guide. Do what is right, even when it hurts.

Report In or You May Be AWOL (Alone and Wandering Out in the Lozone)

People over you will want to know how you're doing. Your coach will ask you questions about your performance and lifestyle and plans. Don't resent it. You need accountability like that. You need to have people asking you the hard questions, or else you'll sluff off and think it doesn't matter. If it matters to them, it will matter to you.